FREE Days Out in Lancashire*
(*and the surrounding areas)

by Garry Cook

All rights reserved.

All images © Copyright Garry Cook 2014
ISBN- 978-1499799606
ISBN-1499799608

Introduction 5
Withy Grove Park, Bamber Bridge................................. 6
The Atom... 8
Darwen Tower and Sunnyhurst Woods......................... 10
Aqua Park at Happy Mount Park, Morecambe 12
Ribchester Park 14
Longridge Fell 16
Clitheroe Castle and skate park.................................... 18
Malham (Not in Lancashire).. 20
Rivington Pike, near Chorley 22
Singing Tree, Crown Point, Burnley.............................. 24
Haslam Park, Preston... 26
Avenham & Miller Park, Preston 28
Brimham Rocks (Not in Lancashire) 30
Edisford Bridge, Clitheroe... 32
Worden Park, Leyland 34
Dunsop Bridge 36
Halo, Haslingden... 38
Pendle Hill steps, Barley side 40
Astley Park, Chorley 42
Beach at Lytham St Annes... 44
Brockholes Nature Reserve 46
Witton Country Park, Blackburn.................................... 48
Formby Point (Not in Lancashire) 50
NOTES.. 52
Extra venue: Gisburn Forest... 53

Introduction

VENUES with car parking fees are not excluded from this list. But any extra costs such as these are included in the summary for every attraction.

Every attraction listed here includes basic hand-drawn maps showing how to get there.

If you are unfamiliar with the recommended attraction, we do suggest you make more detailed notes on how to get there. But as most venues are promoted by the local council and they are usually well sign posted.

There are several venues in this book which are not in Lancashire. I've included them because they are so good I think you need to know about them. Those extra few miles for some amazing days out are really worth it.

This is just the start. There are dozens more great venues in Lancashire. Make your own list or send your suggestions to us. We're on Facebook at www.facebook.com/freedayout

Enjoy the book.

And have a great day out.

Garry Cook

Withy Grove Park, Bamber Bridge

"The best kids playground in Lancashire by a mile"

HIDDEN down the side of an ageing leisure centre is not where you would expect to find Lancashire's greatest playground. But that is exactly what Withy Grove is. Built in 2007 and still looking fresh and clean, the toddler's area is built on masses of sand and has loads of apparatus to climb on and slide down.

There is also a giant twin-poled rope climbing framing, a peculiar carrot-shaped tower with two slides and a series of tougher frames for teenagers. Throw in a zip wire and some lovely little dexterity pieces and you've got a genuine playground paradise. I can't praise this place highly enough.

Better known as the Bamber Bridge playground, this is the ultimate free venue. A huge fenced-off piece of land split into three sections is ideal for all ages. There's even the added bonus of a small skate park next to it. There are also football fields and parkland which is ideal for cycling or walking the dogs.

You can actually see this place from the M6 but you'll need to come off at J29 and head for

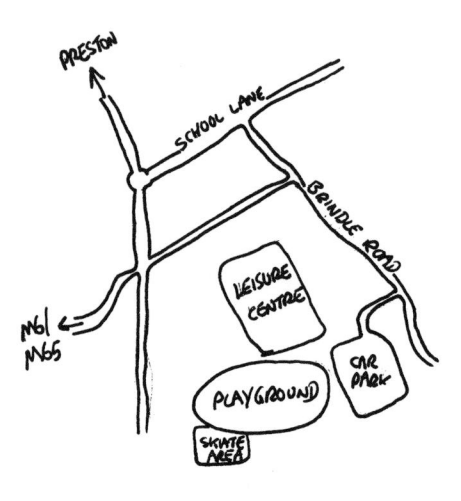

Bamber Bridge on the A6. Take a quick right turn on to the B5257 Brownedge Road which will twist and turn into Brownedge Lane before going straight over at the lights in to Collins Road and then turning right on to Brindle Road. You should be seeing signs for the leisure centre to help you along. There is loads of free parking but on hot sunny days the place is rammed.

Fun rating: 5/5
Activity type: Outdoor play
Duration: Two hours
Age range: 1+
Address: Brindle Rd, Bamber Bridge, Preston, Lancashire PR5 6YJ

What will cost you more?
Car Parking: Free
Food and drinks: I've never actually seen the Leisure Centre Café open. They are missing out on loads of trade

The Atom, Wycoller Country Park

"Public art meets public pathways as the focal point for a lovely circular walk"

THE Panopticons are permanent pieces of public art installed at four different locations in east Lancashire, three of them on top of hills with fantastic views.

The Atom is easily the best of these, a stunning stone structure situated high up on the side of a valley. Coupled with a lovely walk – just as good in winter as summer – and you've got a fantastic day trip.

The Atom is a great place to shelter or eat a picnic. The kids love sitting in the open windows and running around on the hill outside. Sadly, the centre-piece silver ball won't be there. It was hacked off by local hooligans some years ago. In the village itself there are some brilliant bridges to get across and some the ruins of Wycoller Hall explore.

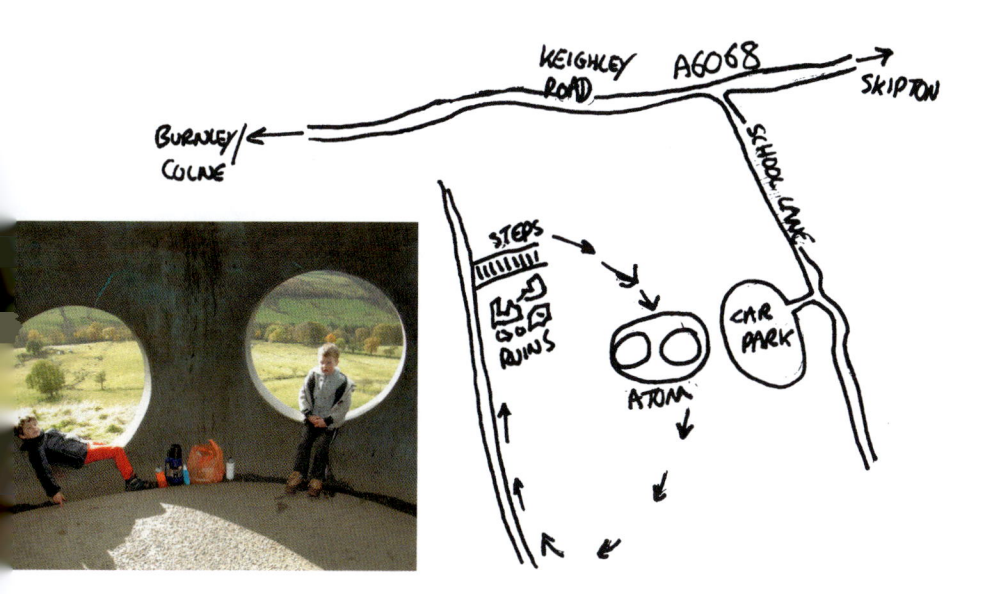

Though parts of the walk are steep and muddy, the route is fairly easy for kids, with enough twists and turns to stop them realising just how far they've walked. The race back up the hill to The Atom can be quite fun if there's a treat on offer at the end.

The Atom is not the easiest to find. From the A6068 Keighley Road turn south on to School Lane and look for the little car park as you drive up the hill. Don't follow signs to Wycoller Country Park which you might see earlier if you are travelling from Colne. Parking right next to The Atom means you can leave your picnic in the car and start walking. The trail, if you initially head south, takes you through someone's garden but don't worry about that, it is a public footpath. Eventually you drop down into the valley. Walk into Wycoller, play in the old ruins, and then walk up the stone steps back up to The Atom.

Fun rating: 4/5
Activity type: Outdoor walking
Duration: Two hours
Address: Laneshawbridge, Colne, BB8 7HX

Age range: 4+
What will cost you more?
Car Parking: Free
Food and drinks: Craft Centre café in Wycoller

Darwen Tower and Sunnyhurst Woods

"Perfect for tiring out energetic kids"

A STEEP walk with great views on the way up and again when you reach the top of the tower. This trek is particularly stunning on summer evenings.

For a shorter walk, start at the car park just past the Sunnyhurst Hotel pub, off Sunnyhurst Lane. Walk west along the road track, keeping left when road splits. Turn left when you see steep trail leading up to Sunnyhurst Hey reservoir. Walk towards the hill and either take a steep direct route to tower through heather or walk east alongside the reservoir and then follow diagonal path up the hill.

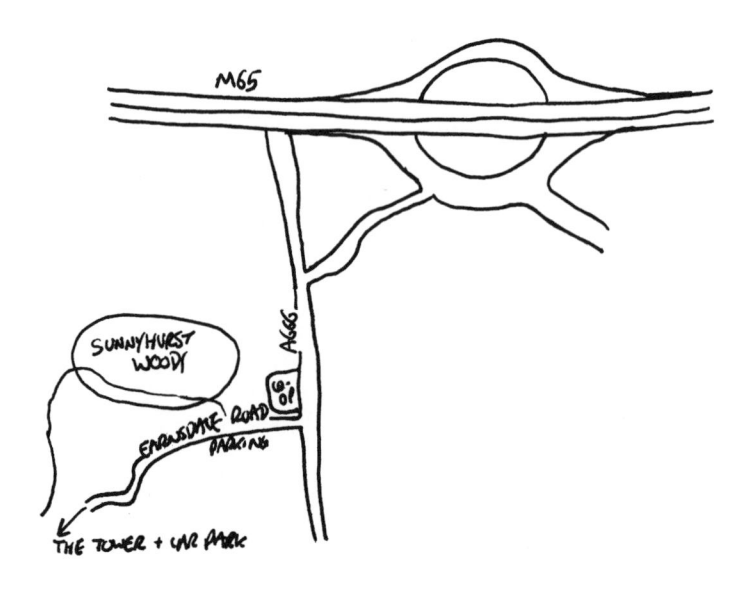

For a longer walk park on Earnsdale Road opposite the entrance to Sunnyhurst Woods. Walk down to the woods and follow the trails until the path rises to the lower Earnsdale Reservoir. Walk along the road then up a short, steep trail to another road track, turn right. Turn left when you see steep trail leading up to Sunnyhurst Hey reservoir.

The walk down from the tower is much quicker. Follow the trail down side of hill which emerges at the Sunnyhurst Hotel.

It's a long walk, so be sure to take some food and drinks for when you reach the Tower. Rest on stone seats with wonderful views across Lancashire.

Fun rating: 4/5
Activity type: Outdoor walking
Duration: Three hours
Age range: 6+ (under 4s & 5s could end up whinging because of the steepness of the hill)
Address: Sunnyhurst Lane, Tockholes Rd, Darwen BB3 1JX
What will cost you more?
Car parking: Free
Food and drinks: Olde English Kiosk in Sunnyhurst Wood

Aqua Park at Happy Mount Park, Morecambe

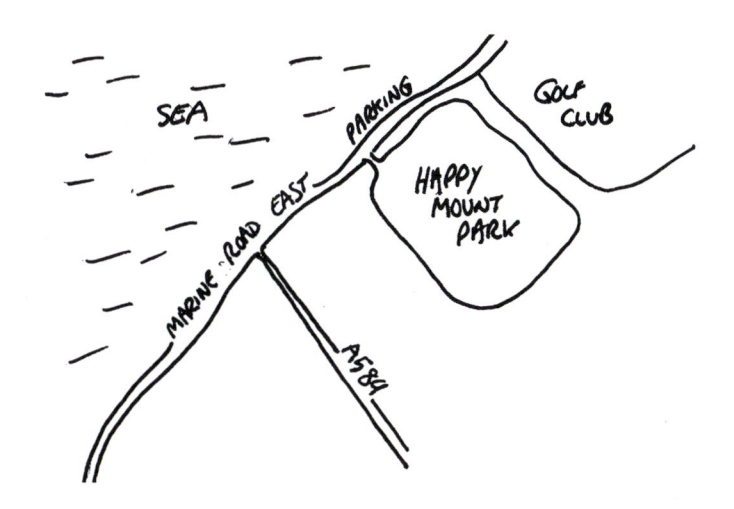

"When the sun is out there is nothing better than splash-park craziness"

HIDDEN in an old-fashioned Victorian park are glorious fountains of fun which drive kids wild.

Parents can watch from the sidelines as the kids delight in enthralling water jets and cascading showers. Even toddlers can get involved with some of the gentler jets on the outskirts of the magnificently designed water installation.

Park on the sea road (Marine Road East) and walk into Happy Mount where the traditional surroundings hide this kid's paradise splash park. Most of the other attractions in the park are paid for, including the indoor Pirates in the Park play centre, the Victorian roundabout and swingboats. But the Aqua Park, easily the stand-out activity at Happy Mount, is free. Be sure to bring a towel and trunks.

Fun rating: 5/5
Activity type: Outdoor play
Duration: Two hours
Age range: 1+
Address: Marine Rd E, Morecambe LA4 5AQ

What will cost you more?
Car Parking: Free
Paid attractions: Several other rides
Food and drinks: Available at Café in the Park

Ribchester Park

"Safe and secure outdoor playground fun will have even the laziest kids working up a sweat."

A TRADITIONAL play ground with an unusual design to keep children running until they are worn out.

This is a firm favourite of ours. Older kids can enjoy a game of football on the grass field or on the hard court next to the play area. Younger ones will be happy to run up and down the hill which forms part of the slide and playing chase around the fantastic climbing frame.

Park opposite the entrance for just 40p if you stay less than an hour. Want to stay longer? The car park is so close you can easily get another ticket while the kids carry on playing in their enclosed space. Park in the village and make the short walk past the café if you don't fancy paying for parking.

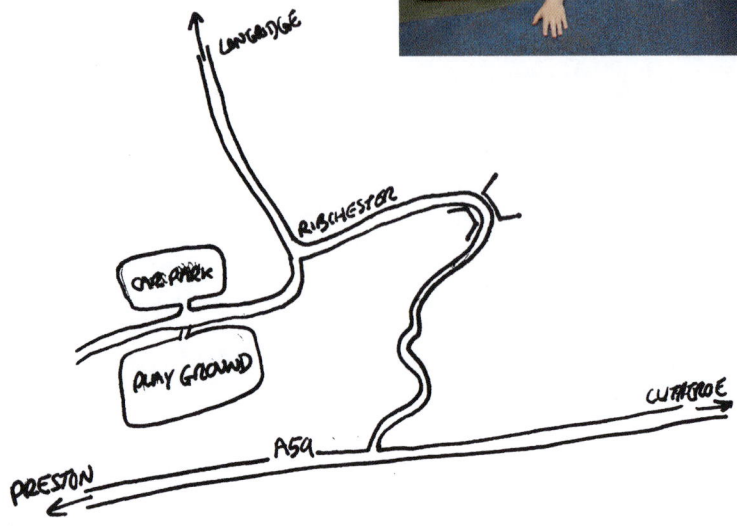

Fun rating: 4/5
Activity type: Outdoor play
Duration: Two hours
Age range: 2+
Address: Church Street, Ribchester, Preston, PR3 3YE
What will cost you more?
Car parking: 40p for one hour **Food and drinks:** Café just down the road, Spar round the corner, ice-cream van at busy periods in summer

Longridge Fell

"Possibly Lancashire's most unused tourist destination"

VARIOUS walks through forests and heather with glorious views of the Forest of Bowland and the Trough of Bowland.

It's easy to cram in dramatic views with shady forest trails, many of which double-up as rarely used mountain-bike trails.

If the kids really don't like walking, then this is probably not for your family. The best walks I've had here are with my daughter in the backpack.

There are various starting points along the Fell, with trails across heathland or thick forest.

An extended walk can be made by going down one of the paths on the steep north face, with a walk back up the hill a little further along. This will push you past the two-hour limit though – and have you sweating on the way back up.

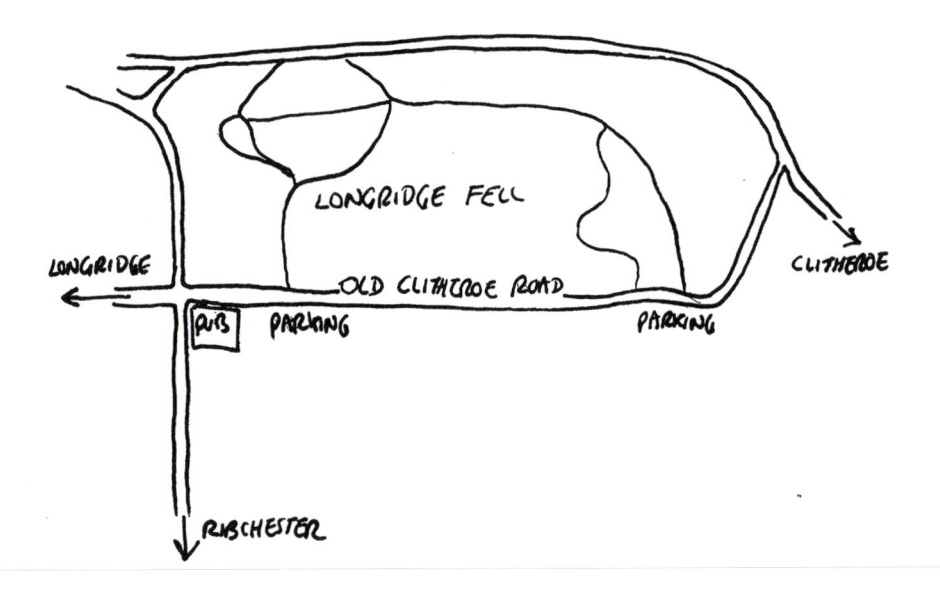

The trig point is a great target for a varied short walk, starting off along the road track on Old Clitheroe Road, though sadly much of the forest has recently been chopped down.

Alternatively, begin your walk on east end of Fell, near Birdy Brow. Walk up the trail eventually coming to a fantastic viewpoint at a clearing in the trees, then take the rubbly road track back down.

Fun rating: 3/5
Activity type: Outdoor walking
Duration: Two hours
Age range: 7+

Address: Longridge Fell, Old Clitheroe Road, PR3 2YX
What will cost you more?
Car Parking: Free

Clitheroe Castle and skate park

"Castle, play area and skate park all within a stone's throw from the town"

THE play area is good without being inspiring but the skate park is where it's at. A fantastic sheet of curving concrete, dips and giant sinks, this arena keeps the BMXers and skaters occupied for hours. We tend to go early in the day with our young kids (when they were aged four to seven) because the language can get a bit fruity once the place fills up with teenagers. By the afternoon the skate area is packed full of kids trying to outdo themselves with their favourite jumps and tricks.

Finding a free parking space on Eshton Terrace or Woone Lane is never a problem. Then there is a short walk up to the skate park. Clitheroe Castle Keep is free for a quick look round – worth it for the views – but the food in the castle restaurant was pretty poor when we tried it (main menu and the kids meals) and is best avoided. If you've not packed a picnic, you're much better off heading into Clitheroe itself where there are some superb food houses.

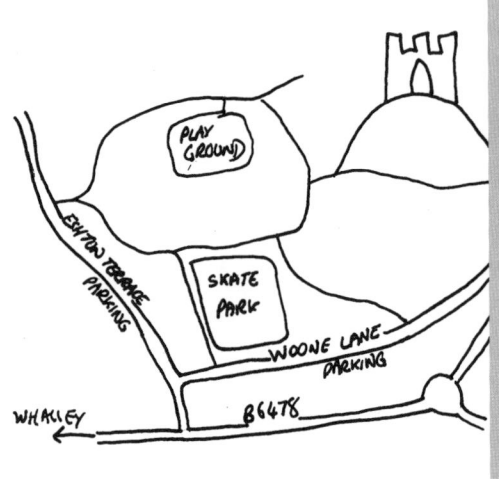

Fun rating: 4/5
Activity type: Outdoor play
Duration: One hour
Age range: 8+
Address: Clitheroe Castle, BB7 1BA
What will cost you more?
Car parking: Free street parking on road to south and west of park grounds
Paid attractions: Castle Museum £3.65 adults/£2.90 kids
Food and drinks: Avoid the Castle restaurant

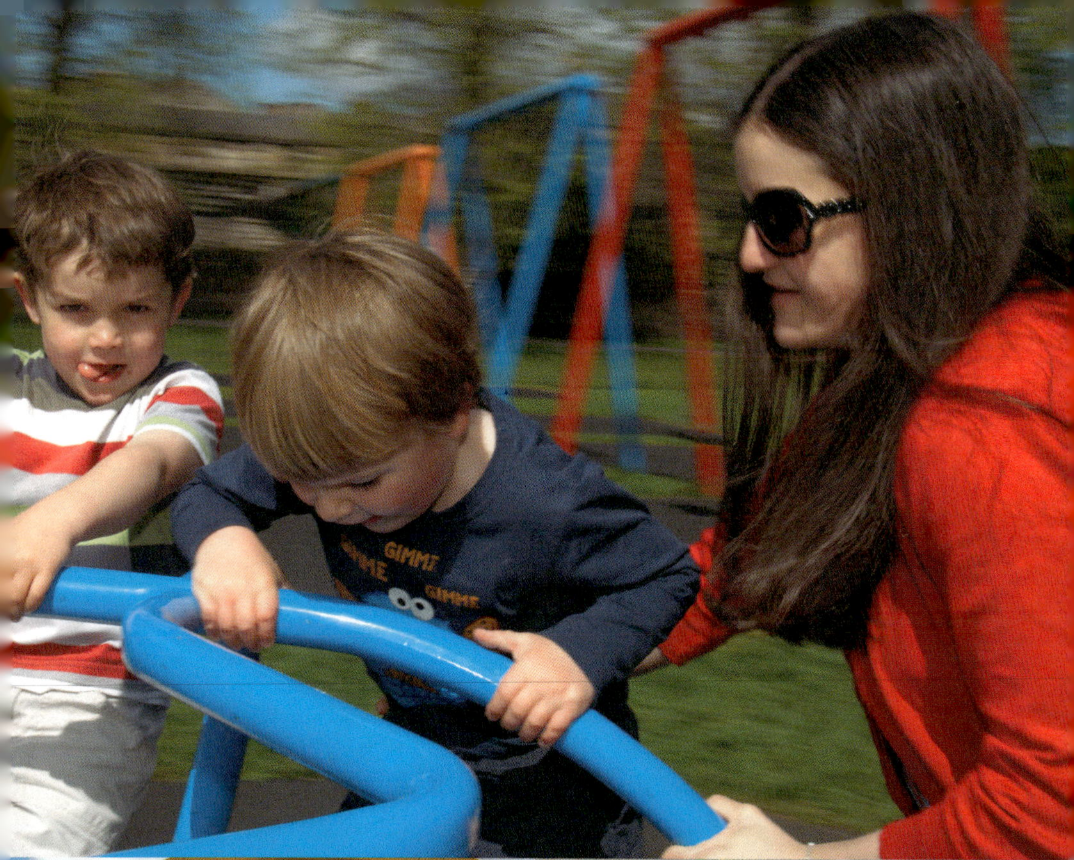
GIMME
GIMME
GIMME

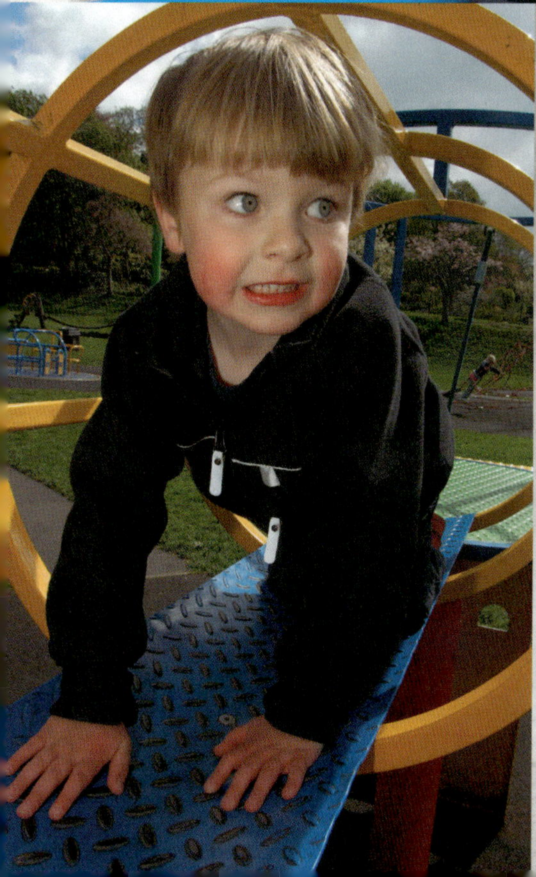

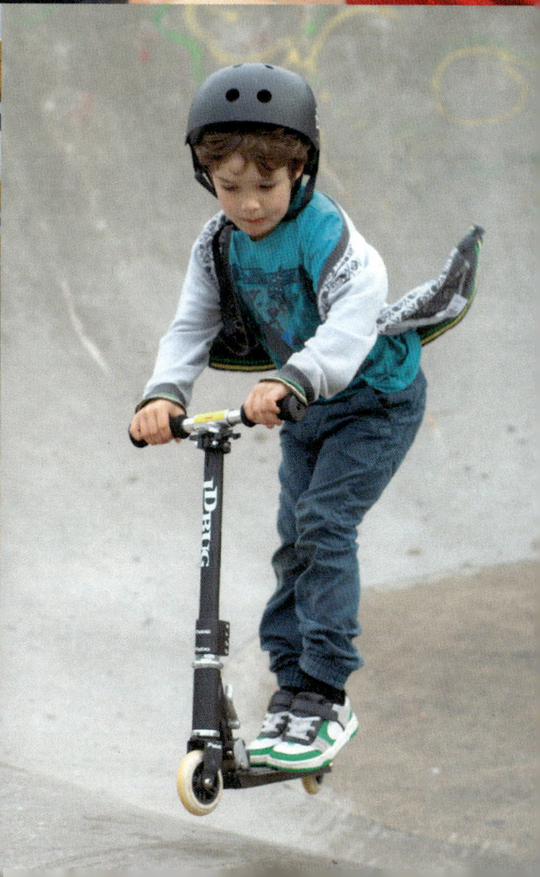

Malham (Not in Lancashire)

"Wonderful walk by a stream turns into a kids climbing day in a rocking rocky valley"

ONCE you are across the stream opposite the car park, follow the path which eventually bends round into Little Goredale Wood and Stony Bank Wood. We even hitched a ride off 77-year-old farmer John Simpson after he allowed us to pile into his quadbike trailer with his dog Nell.

But this is where the fun starts. The wood is magical. The kids love the huge try trunk which has been hammered with coins. And there are even some fascinating information boards to read. After emerging from the woods there is a short walk – with the possibility of a hot drink if the food van is there – to the entrance of Goredale Scar.

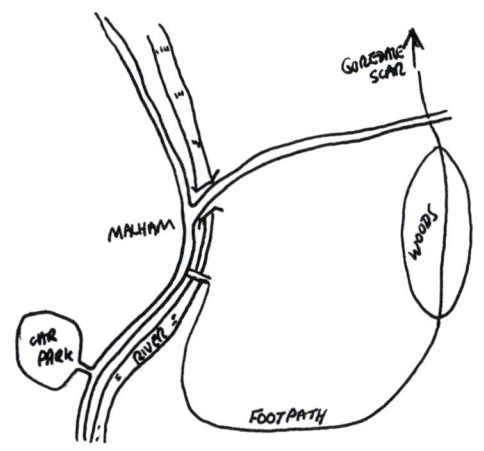

This valley is awesome, ending with a rocky waterfall which many climbers try and fail to clamber up. Attempting this is too much for kids but there is plenty of climbing to be done before returning down the valley and taking the road back into the village.

Older kids can take the footpath up the hill which eventually leads to the top of the magnificent Malham Cove. Then walk down the steps back to the village and car.

Fun rating: 5/5
Activity type: Outdoor walking/outdoor play
Duration: Two to three hours
Age range: 3+
Address: Malham, near Gargrave, North Yorkshire, BD23 4DA
What will cost you more?

Car parking: £4 at the Yorkshire Dales National Park Centre – or try your luck in the village
Food and drinks: Pub and The Old Barn Cafe in Malham village. There may also be a mobile food trailer at the entrance to Goredale Scar

21

Rivington Pike, near Chorley

"A hillside forest walk of steps and bridges which create a real sense of adventure"

RIVINGTON PIKE is a maze of walkways, paths and bridges hidden within a forest on Winter Hill. Strictly speaking the pike is the hill summit – but it's the paths hidden below which bring out the adventurer in young explorers. The Pike Tower on top of the hill is a great destination in the summer months but there's no need to go right to the top if the weather is not so good.

Built by Lord Lever and gifted, along with Lever Park, to the people of Bolton over 100 years ago, some of the buildings in Rivington Pike are slightly worse for wear. A few too many late night summer parties by those pesky teenagers from Chorley leaving some structures boarded up. But that won't detract from the cleverness of the place – making walking up a hill fun.

The path to the hill leads directly from the car park, just off Belmont Road. Don't leave any valuables in your car as thieves have targeted this car park in the past, though you should be okay at busy times. Make sure you all stick together because the pathways and bridges are a bit of a maze and it's easy to get lost.

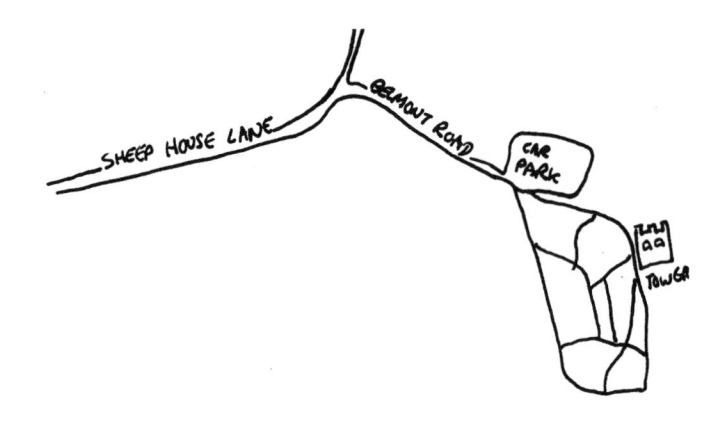

Fun rating: 3/5
Activity type: Outdoor walking
Duration: 90 minutes
Address: Belmont Road,
Rivington BL6 7RZ (nearest)
Age range: 5+
What will cost you more?
Car Parking: Free

Singing Tree, Crown Point, Burnley

"Science meets art in a country setting where a tubular metal tree whistles in the wind."

THE kids will not forget their visit to the Singing Tree for a long time, even though that visit will be quite brief. So it's good if you are a beginner at family walks in the country.

Situated high on the hillside south of Burnley, the swirl of metal tubes serves up a tuneful backing track to some fantastic views. The short and - if it's windy - exposed walk from the car park means your visit will

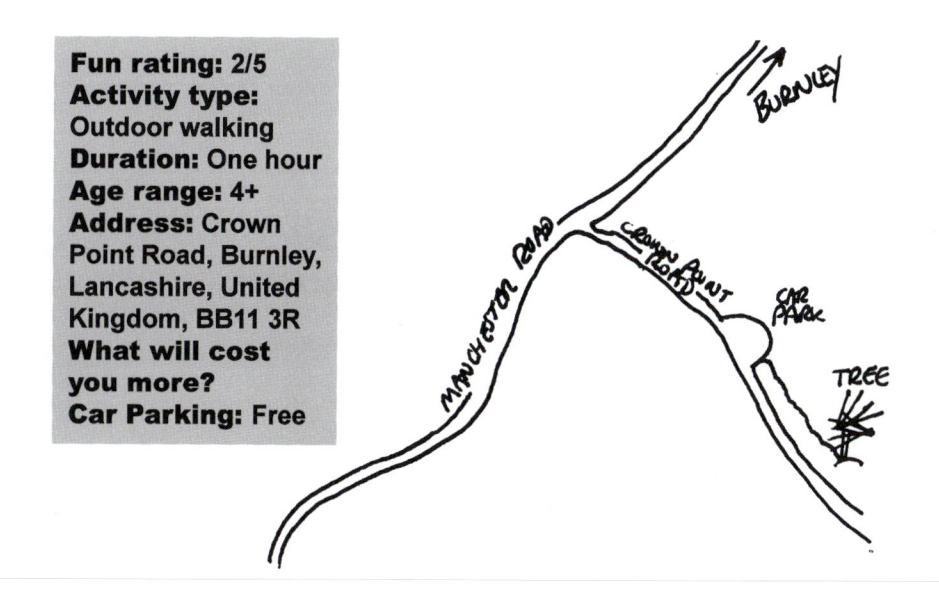

Fun rating: 2/5
Activity type: Outdoor walking
Duration: One hour
Age range: 4+
Address: Crown Point Road, Burnley, Lancashire, United Kingdom, BB11 3R
What will cost you more?
Car Parking: Free

struggle to last over an hour. But it's worth it because this brilliant artwork is so unusual.

If you want to make the visit longer you could try walking across one of the trails from Clowbridge Reservoir on the A682 Manchester Road, eventually crossing Crown Point Road and walking down to the Panopticon. It's a great walk for older kids.

Look for the half-circle shaped car park side of Crown Point Road. You can see the Singing Tree from there.

Haslam Park, Preston

"One hundred years after first opening, the Victorian brilliance still shines through"

LUSH green parks are the best thing about Preston and Haslam Park does not disappoint, with a lovely lake and canal often so packed with wildfowl you won't be able to count them all. The long boulevard-style walk from the main gates down the west of the park is stunning in all seasons.

The playground, near the entrance, is for younger kids but the nearby tennis courts are in good condition and are free. The flat and mostly wide paths are great for young cyclists. It's easy to extend your walk by going on to the canal tow path. If you head south it comes to an abrupt end halfway to Preston and is a bit rundown. Go north and it is in a much better condition, with some lovely back gardens to nosey at. The best route is to head north over the bridge in the park itself, walk over the meadow and when you reach the footbridge over the canal, turn right.

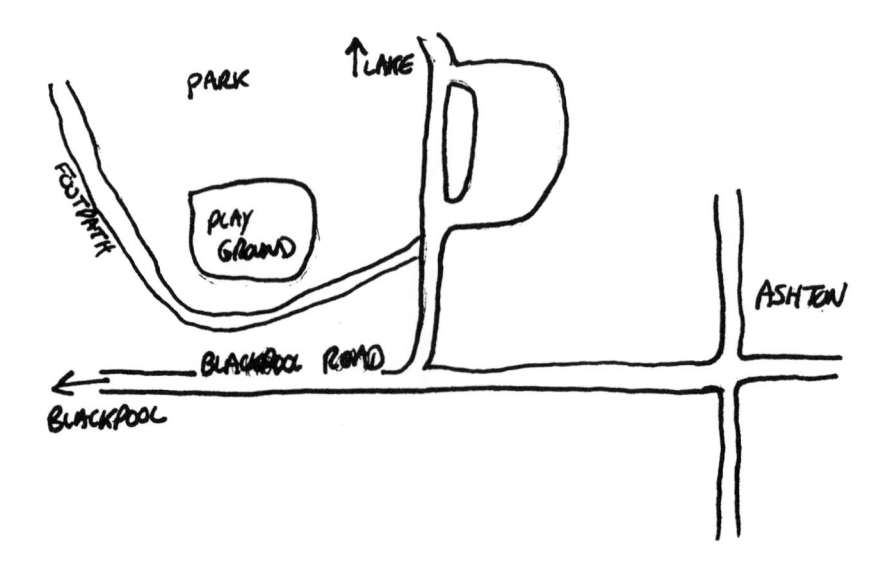

Access to the park is not ideal as Blackpool Road has a central reservation – meaning you can only turn into it if heading east. If you are coming from Ashton centre (heading west) turning round is not ideal, though is possible after the bridge. On the park be aware of the occasional slow-moving vehicles heading to the allotments just over the bridge. The car park is fairly small and gets busy on summer weekend afternoons.

Fun rating: 2/5
Activity type: Outdoor walking/ outdoor play
Duration: One hour
Age range: 1+

Address: Blackpool Road, Preston, PR2 1JE
What will cost you more?
Car Parking: Free

Avenham and Miller Park, Preston

"Restored Victorian splendour close to the city but so much better"

JUST a few years ago these two parks – commonly referred to as just Avenham Park – were forgotten relics, overgrown, rundown and dirty. Some major refurbishment has restored both beyond their former glories, making them easily the best thing about Preston.

Hidden away at the southern end of Avenham Park, just over the hill past the low bridge, is a small children's playground.

You feel like you are walking out of the park to get there but just keep going – keeping on the path which hugs the River Ribble – and you will get there.

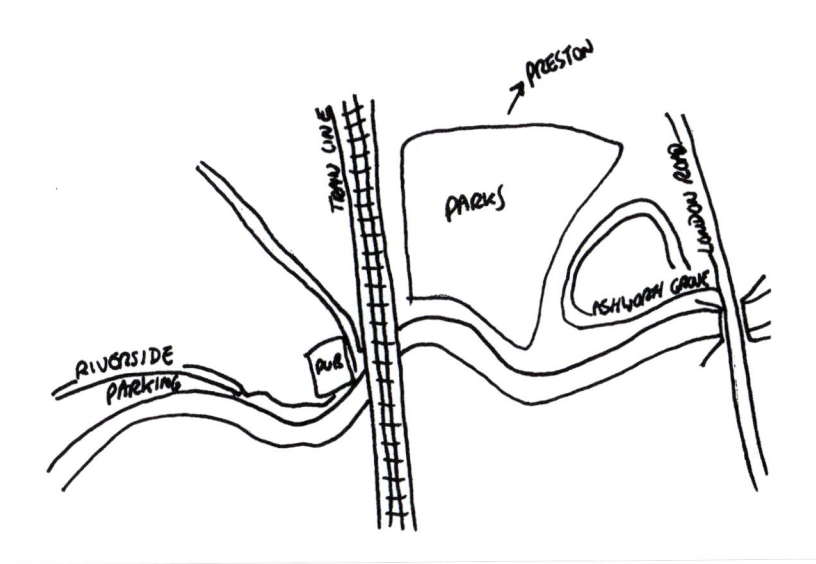

Miller Park, with its huge circular fountain and Victorian steps, is an ideal place for a picnic. But there's also a modern designed café in Avenham Park close to the beautifully restored Japanese gardens.

Extend your walk by venturing over one of the bridges, though this longer route is much better by bike.

For those who prefer a longer walk or cycle, park near Vernon Carus Cricket Club in Lower Penwortham and walk/cycle along one of two pathways and bridges into the parks. The pathway from the Continental pub (another parking option but which is very busy during weekdays) also doubles up as part of the Guild Wheel cycle route, a 20-odd mile city loop.

You can also park in the housing estate accessed from the other side of Preston on London Road, turn on to Ashworth Grove just next to Walton Bridge.

Fun rating: 3/5
Activity type: Outdoor play/outdoor walking
Duration: 90 minutes
Age range: 1+

Address: Preston, Lancashire PR1 8JT
What will cost you more?
Car parking: Free **Food and drinks:** Riverside Café

Brimham Rocks (Not in Lancashire)

"You won't believe your eyes when you see the balancing rock formations"

A NATURAL playground of stunning rock formations within a picturesque forest. If I mention the words 'Brimham Rocks' in our house, excitement levels reach fever pitch. One of the best days out ever.

There are enough nooks, crannies and boulders to entertain the kids for hours. The labyrinth-like natural layout means no two visits are ever the same. Little kids will love exploring and squeezing through tiny tunnels. Teenagers will have just as much fun scaling some of the bigger rock formations. Some of the best views across the valley come from rocks you don't even have to climb, meaning the entire family can join in – even granny and grandad.

You can lose yourselves in the maze of rocks – but you can't actually get lost. The natural layout of the Millstone Grit rocks is easily navigated thanks to a couple of wide footpaths which act as a pointer to the centre of the park. All paths eventually lead to a picnic area, with tea cabin serving drinks, snacks and ice cream. Go up over the other side of the valley for more amazing rock formations.

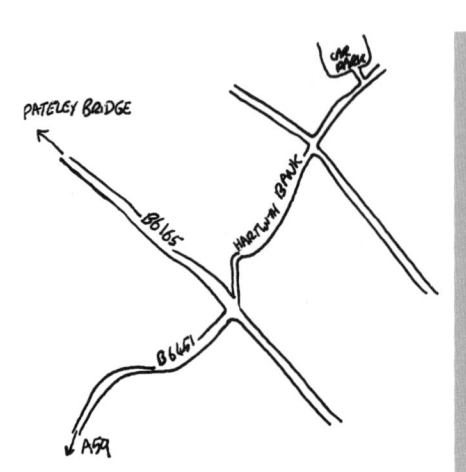

Fun rating: 5/5
Activity type: Outdoor play
Duration: Three hours
Age range: 4+ (Ideal for teens)
Address: Ripon Road Barn Blazefield, Pateley Bridge, Ripon, Yorkshire HG3 4DW
What will cost more?
Car parking: £4 for three hours (free for NT members)
Food and drinks: Tea, Coffee and Ice-cream available at the kiosk

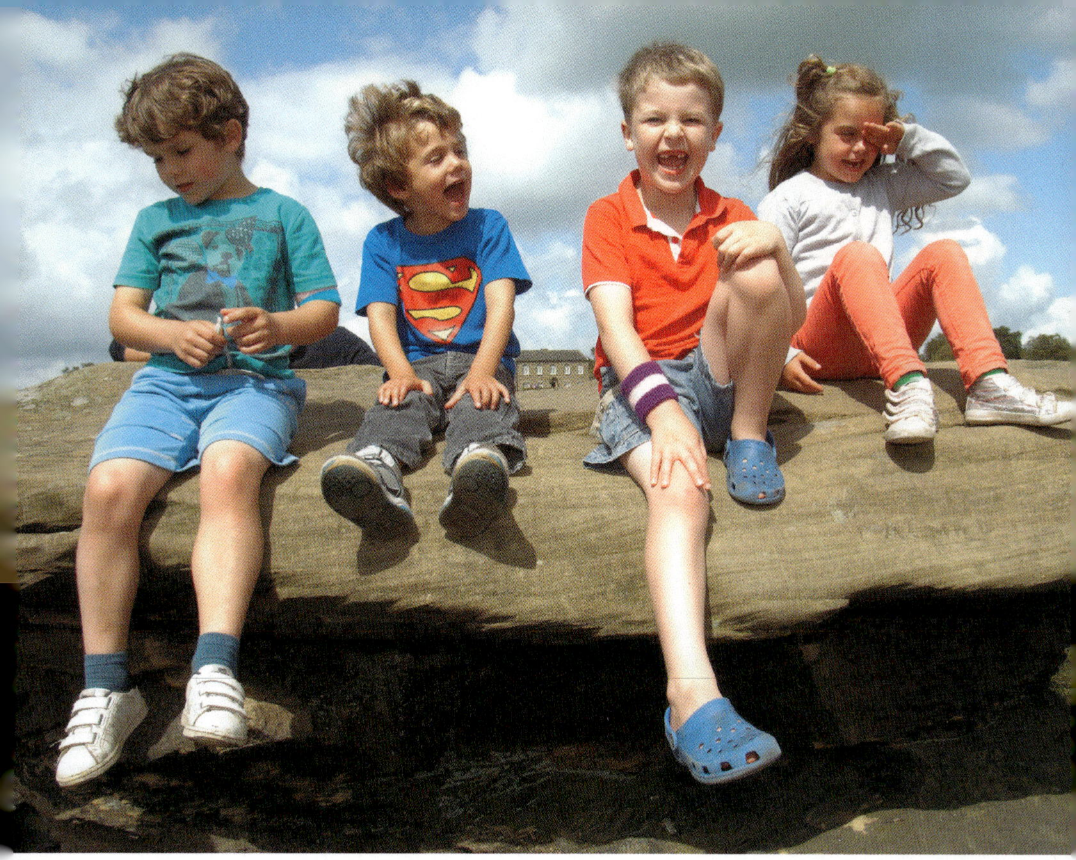

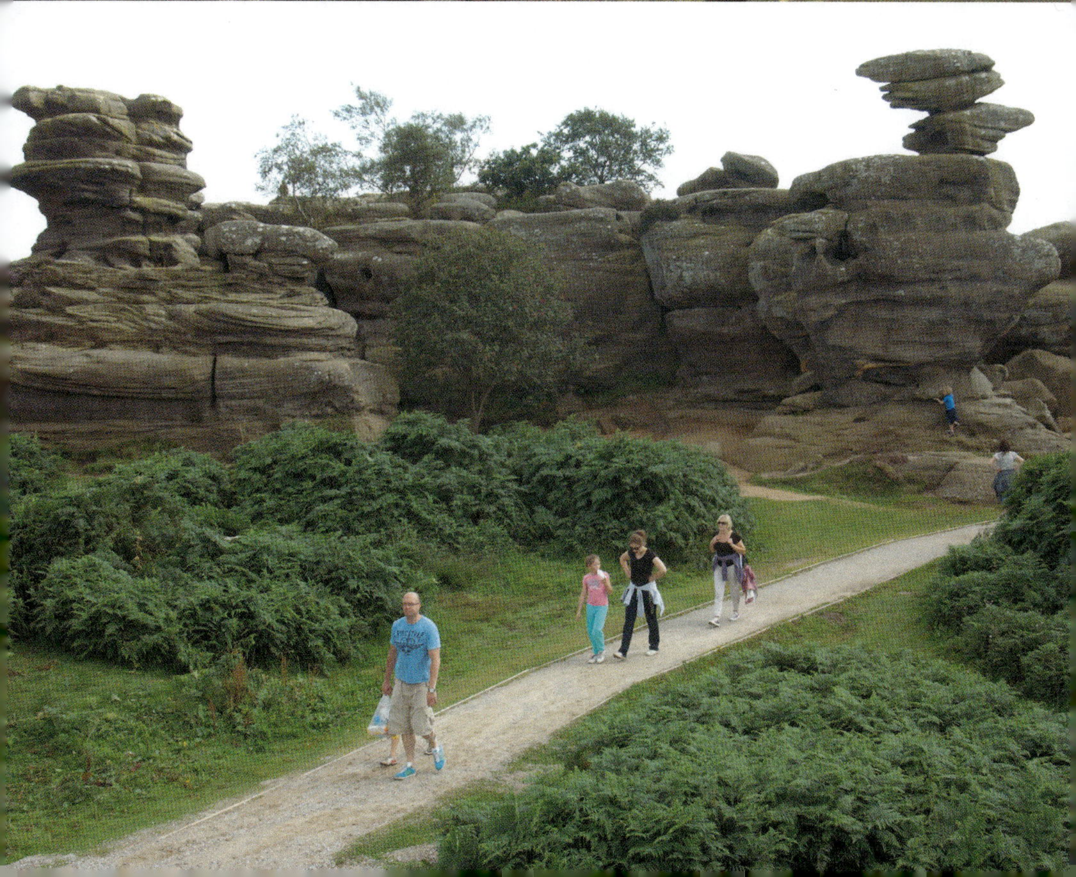

Edisford Bridge, Clitheroe

"Kids will get wet and wild in the river before pestering you to get in the queue for an ice-cream"

A LOVELY stretch of water next to a grass field perfect for ball games make this area a honeypot for young families. And with clean water, rocks to climb and grass verges to lie on, it's easy to see why.

IIt's a five-minute walk from the car park to the stream, so make sure you don't leave anything in the car. With a picnic, ball, towels and tennis racquets, you may feel like a wobbly pack horse on the walk down. The current in the stream can be deceivingly strong in some parts so do not let under-8s go in the water alone. I did have to perform a rescue mission on one of the kids when he was five and got into a bit of difficulty in the water.

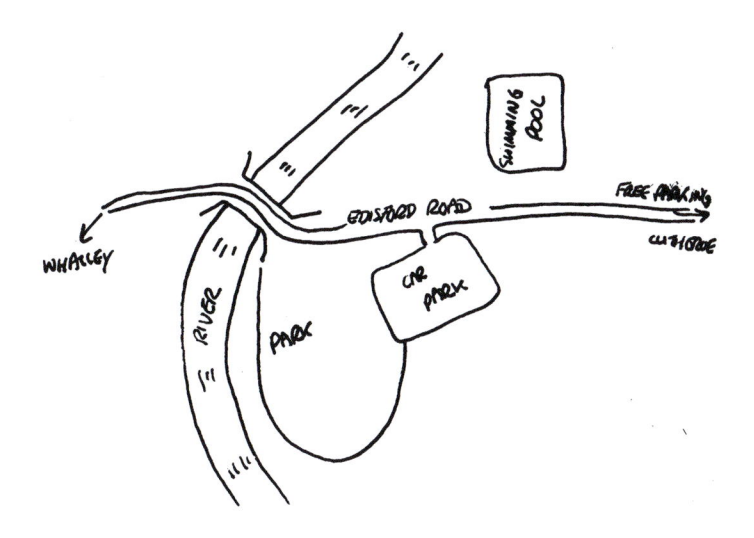

But the big drawback is car parking charges and traffic wardens who verge on the obsessive - so make sure you pay and don't park across the white lines or you will get done. As we did.

Summer Sunday afternoons (providing the weather is good) sees the miniature railway in full swing.

If the weather turns bad the swimming pool is across the road.

Fun rating: 3/5
Activity type: Outdoor play
Duration: Two to three hours
Age range: 4+
Address: Edisford Road, Clitheroe BB7 3LJ

What will cost you more?
Car parking: £1.80 for three hours
Food and drinks: Hot days usually bring out the ice-cream van

Worden Park, Leyland

"Playground, fields, woods and stream, everything you need for a mini-adventure day out"

WORDEN Park is the hidden gem of Leyland with fantastic tree-lined walkways, a stream shallow enough for kids to have a paddle in and a delightfully unusual playgroud. There's even a maze and a grass tennis court (though I've never seen it being used). A one hour walk includes wooden bridges, ponds, tracks and enough twists and turns to keep the kids entertained. Summer Sunday mornings are the best time to go where you can time the end of your walk with the first ride of the day on the free miniature railway which chugs round in a lovely loop.

Most of the paths are flat and wide, ideal for tentative learner cyclists (but don't take the bikes on the forest trail down by the stream). The large playground is a mixture of unusual old equipment and some decent new pieces.

Weekends are obviously the busiest period but the amateur

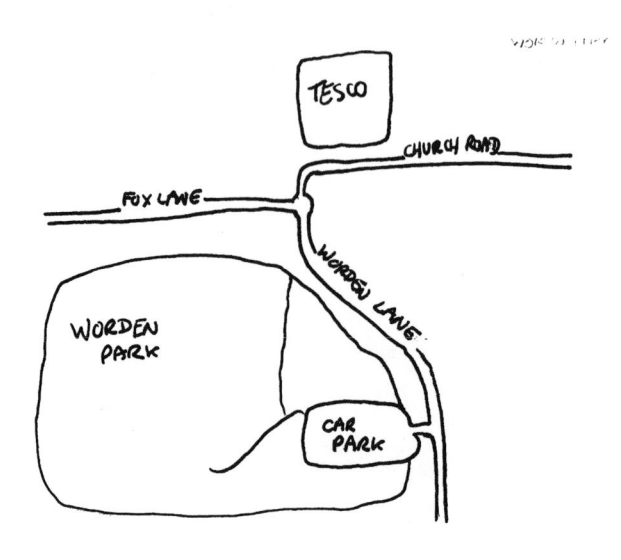

football match kick-offs at 11am make parking that little bit more difficult, and while there is an over-floor car park on the grass. The north entrance (closest to the town) is a lovely way to come into the park, though you can no longer park outside this gate. Worden is very popular with dog walkers so keep an eye on younger children though most owners are very responsible.

Fun rating: 4/5
Activity type: Outdoor play/outdoor walking
Duration: 90 minutes
Age range: 1+
Address: Worden Lane, Leyland, PR25 3DH

What will cost you more?
Car parking: Free (but three-hour maximum stay)
Paid attractions: Train rides are free but there is a donation box
Food and drinks: Small café in the centre of the park

Country walk & ducks, Dunsop Bridge

"Return to nature with a beautiful isolated valley for walking and cycling"

BEING the centre of Britain is one of Dunsop Bridge's best-kept secrets. And so is it's long, flat, quiet country lane which serves as Lancashire's best cycling route for kids.

Just park in the village, down the side of Puddleducks Café next to the Bridge (pretty much all there is in the village) and head north.

The road goes over a couple of cattle grates, round the back of a cluster of houses and then over the rive via a cute little wooden bridge. Then it's north again along a lovely smooth, flat road with only sheep to

Fun rating: 5/5
Activity type: Outdoor walking/cycling
Duration: Two hours
Age range: 4+
Address: Dunsop Bridge, Clitheroe BB7 3BB
What will cost you more?
Car Parking: Free
Food and drink: Puddleducks Cafe

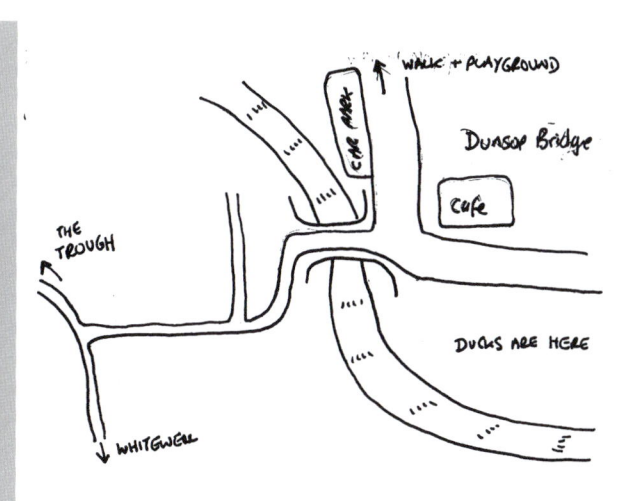

dodge. Occasionally a vehicle may come along, but usually travelling at such slow speed that there is rarely a problem.

After passing some waterworks buildings the road eventually goes up a hill and splits in two, heading off to a couple of very remote farms. If you've got older kids, you can carry on but the younger ones will be happy to stop for a picnic or treat, have a bit of a run around, and then head back to Dunsop Bridge where there is a very good playground.

Ice cream at the café is an optional extra but feeding the ducks is compulsory – and you won't ever meet friendlier ducks. They are very eager for food.

Halo, Haslingden

"Must be seen at dusk for its illuminated splendour against a backdrop of spectacular views"

I'VE seen Halo described as 'an 18m-diameter steel lattice structure supported on a tripod'. I prefer to think of it as a giant fruit bowl on stilts. Either way it is quite impressive, especially at dusk when its electric blue lights come on.

Halo is high up on the hillside above Haslingden. The road up to it is narrow, very steep - and parking space is tight.

The Panopticon is next to a series of pathways through forest and open grassland.

Despite the views, the walks are fairly uninspiring. But Halo is a great destination to take the kids if you want a bit of fresh air and not much exercise.

Go up the hill (from High Street) on Higher Lane and turn right on to Cribden End Lane. Park as the road bends round after you've passed Halo on your left.

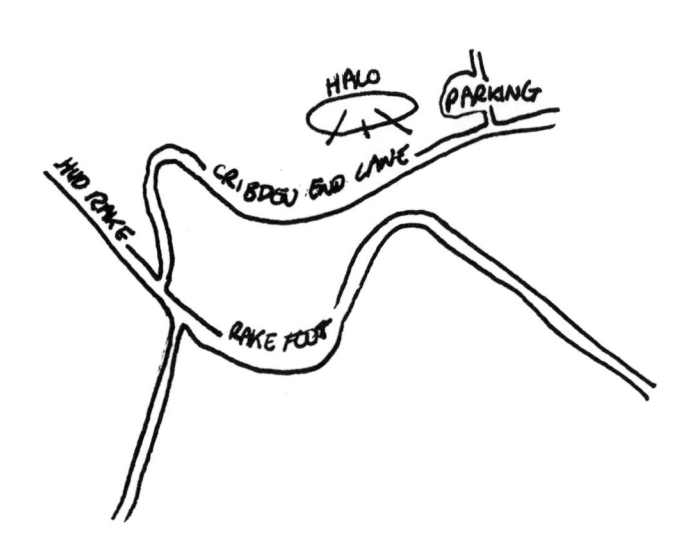

Fun rating: 2/5
Activity type: Outdoor walking
Duration: Two hours
Age range: 4+

Address: Cribden End Lane, Haslingden, Rossendale, BB4 8UB
What will cost you more?
Car Parking: Free

Pendle Hill steps, Barley

"Steep stone steps reward you with stunning views across Lancashire"

PENDLE HILL is the place where the witches of Lancashire used to hang out 400 years ago. If I don't agree with their politics, I certainly agree with their views – which are stunning once you reach the top. The kids do find the walk tough but everybody is delirious with a sense of achievement when they reach the top.

You can choose to park in the picturesque village of Barley and take a 30-minute walk along footpaths and trails to the foot of the hill. The car park is cheap – but there is roadside parking in the village or even directly outside the car park, though this does get busy at weekends. The reward for this longer walk is a treat at the quaint little cabin on the car park or the fabulous homely cafe situated in the row of cottages. For a shorter walk drive north out of Barley and park on the hillside where the road widens next to a farm track which leads almost directly to the steps.

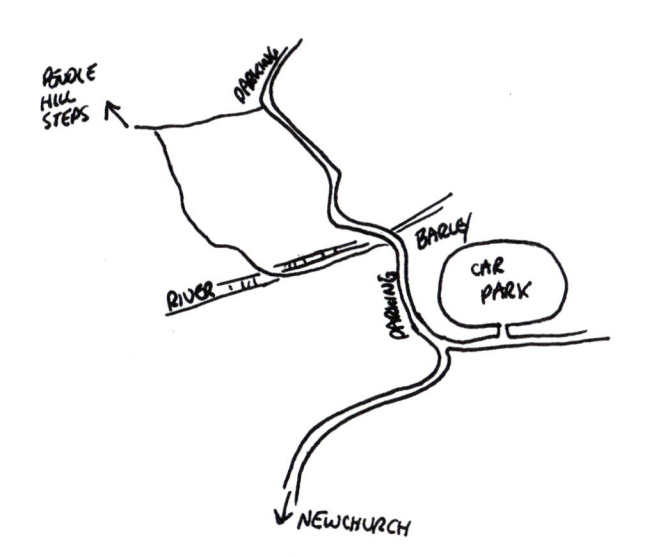

The roads to Barley are narrows and winding whether you come from the A59 near Clitheroe (through Chatburn and Downham) or from the Burnley side (from Padiham or Read through Newchurch).

Fun rating: 3/5
Activity type: Outdoor walking
Duration: Two hours
Age range: 6+ (or you might end up carrying them)
Address: Barley, BB12 9JT

What will cost you more?
Car Parking: Free
Food and drinks: Enjoy the fabulous cafe in the village of the hut on the car park after your walk

Astley Park, Chorley

"Pet's Corner is an unusual attraction tiny tots will love"

HIDDEN between Chorley town centre and a housing estate, Astley Park is not an obvious destination. But with some decent grass land and forest walks, plus a mini-animal enclosure next to the small playground, it's a great day out for toddlers. Adults will probably get more from the Walled Garden than the kids will.

The forest walk is a little dull and the lake is uninspiring but there is plenty of space for a kickaround.

Astley Hall itself has very limited opening times, including half-term and summer holidays (usually noon until 4pm but please check before you travel). But it is free to get in.

There is a free car park behind the shops at Astley Village, which is easy to find of you're coming from the M61 (J7) or Euxton. From the B2552 Euxton Lane, turn on to Chancery Road and look for the shops. It's a short walk from there to the park. If you are arriving on foot, the park is not that far from Chorley train and bus stations. Just look for the entrance gates on the A581 Park Road.

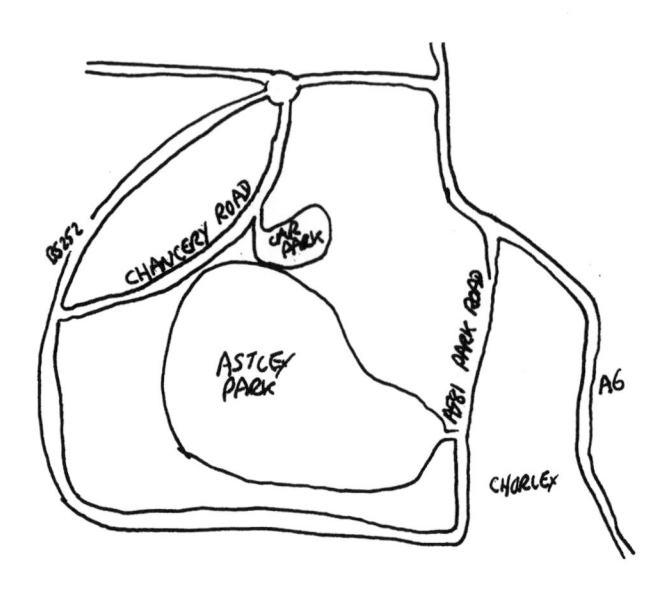

Fun rating: 2/5
Activity type: Outdoor play/walking
Duration: 90 minutes
Address: Chorley, Lancashire PR7 1NP

Age range: 1 to 6
What will cost you more?
Car parking: Free
Food and drinks: Café at next to Astley Hall, kiosk next to Pet's Corner

Beach at Lytham St Annes

"A sandy haven squeezed in between Blackpool's concrete carpet and St Annes' Victorian playground"

THERE'S not much to shout about when it comes to beaches in Lancashire. Formby Point, just into Merseyside, boasts the best beach and dunes in the entire north west. But this short stretch at St Annes, just south of Blackpool, is as close as Lancashire gets to beach paradise. But don't bother if it's not sunny.

When the tide is out the sea can be a very long way away. Which is not necessarily a bad thing as this bit of coastline has dubious water quality. The dunes aren't huge but the sand is perfect for beach games and a picnic. On a hot sunny day, sitting on the soft sand which hugs the dunes, this place almost feels like bliss. It's a great escape from the hard promenade at Blackpool.

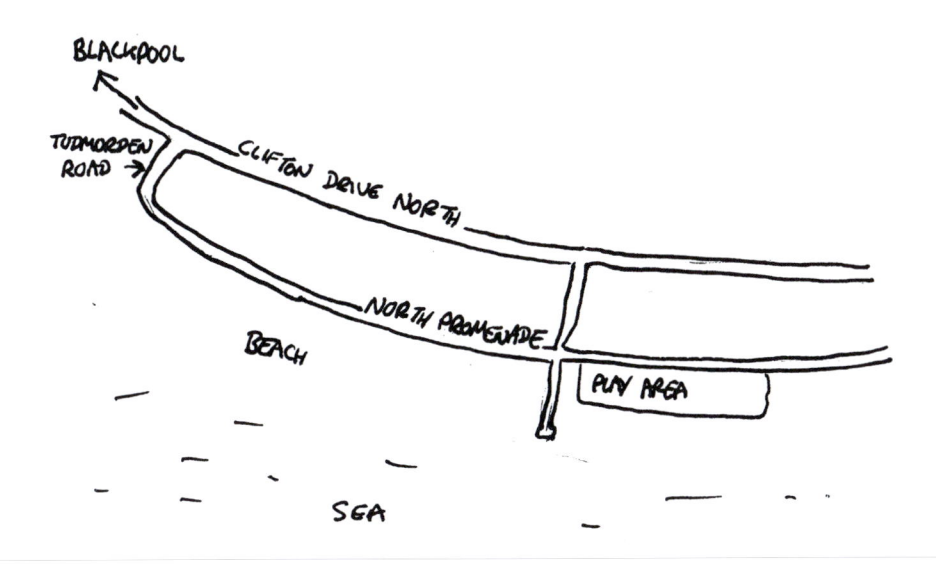

If you take a stroll southwards past the pier you come to the beautiful maze-like stone gardens at St Annes. But be aware – this is where your wallet could take a hit. Trampolines, miniature train, peddle boats, inflatable play area and ice creams all cost pounds, while Ashton Gardens is just across the road. Park for free on the North Promenade road just off the A584. Easiest access is from Blackpool, turning off the A584 Clifton Drive on to Todmorden Road and then North Promenade.

Fun rating: 2/5
Activity type: Outdoor play
Duration: Two hours
Age range: 1+
Address: North Promenade, Lytham St Annes, Lancashire
FY8 2QL
What will cost you more?
Car parking: Free
Paid attractions: Several
Food and drinks: Cafe and shop on pier

Brockholes Nature Reserve

"Magical floating village in an unusual nature reserve and a great cycling destination if you live in Preston!"

KIDS get excited by the 'floating village' but the reality is that unless you are going to eat in the café there is little to do in the floating complex. In my experience the appeal of bird watching for a five year old is pretty much zero. They do put on some crafty things during school half-term (pre-booking is almost essential) but these are generally more expensive than what you will find at most council-run museums.

The outside seating on the floating village is ideal for a picnic.

The adventure play area is the biggest attraction for the kids, with rope bridges for the older ones and more traditional slide and swings for younger children. And there some great are wooded walks with plenty of surprises.

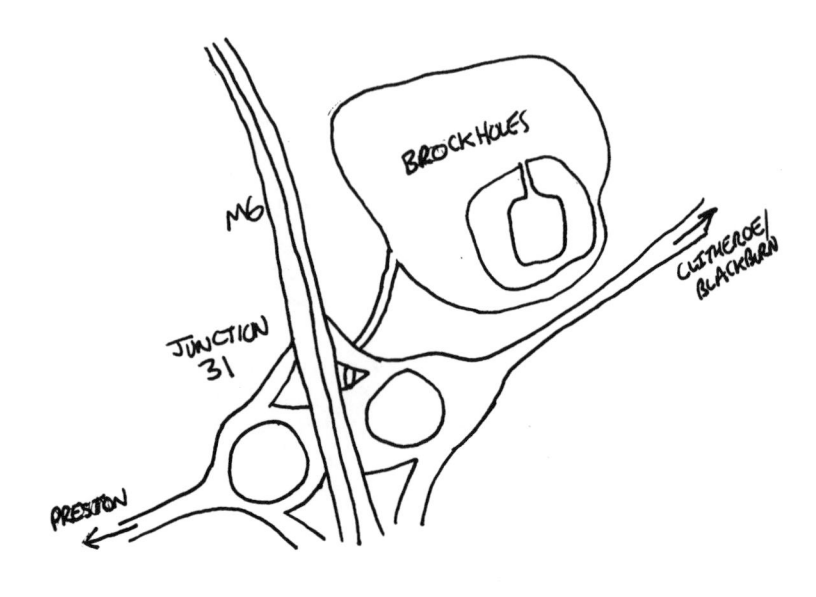

There are also plenty of great trails for walks and bikes – with Preston's Guild Wheel cycling route actually going through the reserve. And cycling, from London Road in Preston, is the best way to approach Brockholes if you live in the city.

Alternatively, take bikes for younger kids (ages three to five) and let them pedal around the paths of Brockholes which sweep around the top of the main parking area.

Fun rating: 3/5
Activity type: Outdoor play
Duration: 90 minutes
Age range: 3+
Address: Junction 31, M6 Samlesbury, Preston, PR5 0AG

What will cost you more?
Car parking: £2 per hour, then 35p per twenty minutes (calculated by vehicle registration recognition system)
Food and drink: The Brockholes restaurant

Witton Country Park, Blackburn

"A monster of a tree-house connected by rope bridges"

WALKING past the immaculate running track you don't expect to find what is a playground paradise through the trees at the end of the lane. But it's a great surprise for the older kids. In front of the centre-piece attraction are loads of other wooden swings and mini-bridges.

The park itself is quite a size but the truth is it will be difficult to drag any six-year-old away from the climbing-frame fun.

Toddlers have their play area in an older, fenced off section next to the running track. Unfortunately this is a short distance away from the main, newer, play area. So if you've got a mixed aged group of kids, this park is not ideal.

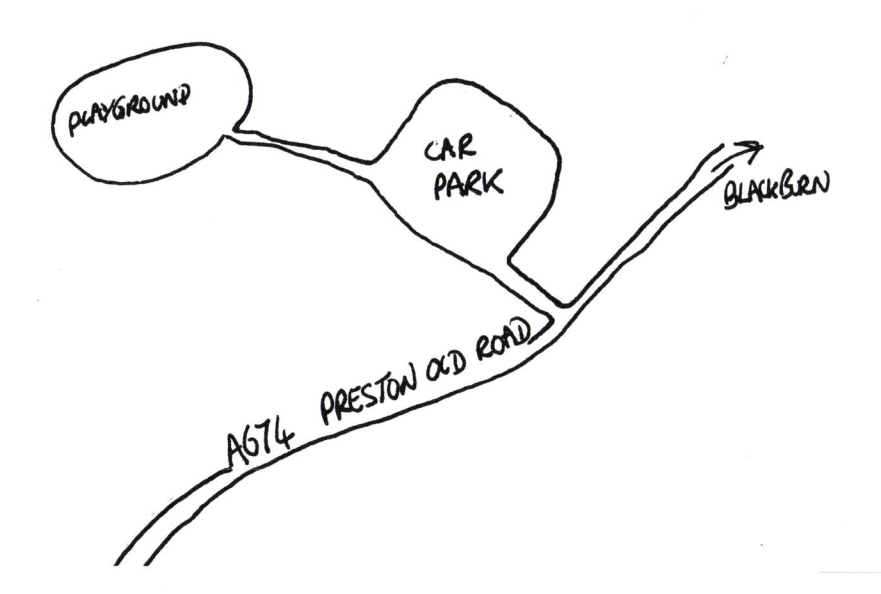

The on-site car park just a few hundred metres from the play area – and don't forget your drinks/supplies as you head off in search of fun. Make sure you tell the kids to be careful in the tree-house part of the play area. I once saw a four-year take a backwards tumble down one of the steep ladders. It was one of those Ouch! moments you don't want to see again in a hurry.

Fun rating: 4/5
Activity type: Outdoor play
Duration: 60 minutes
Age range: 4+

Address: Preston Old Rd, Blackburn, BB2 2TP
What will cost you more?
Car parking: Free **Food and drinks:** Pavilion Cafe

Formby Point (Not in Lancashire)

"The best stretch of beach on the north west coast, amazing sand dunes and friendly squirrels"

HUGE, huge, huge sand dunes stretch as far as the eye can see. And these sand mounds are a kid's dream for climbing up, jumping off and rolling down. When the weather is good, there is no better place to be in the north west.

Like most of this coastline, when the tide is out it is a long way out. Sometimes you can't even see the sea. But when it is close to dunes there is fun to be had as the water swells in, forming shrinking sand islands which excite the kids until the entire family is forced to wade through the water for dry land. Paddling is safe but please do not let the kids swim in the Irish Sea as the water is just not clean enough.

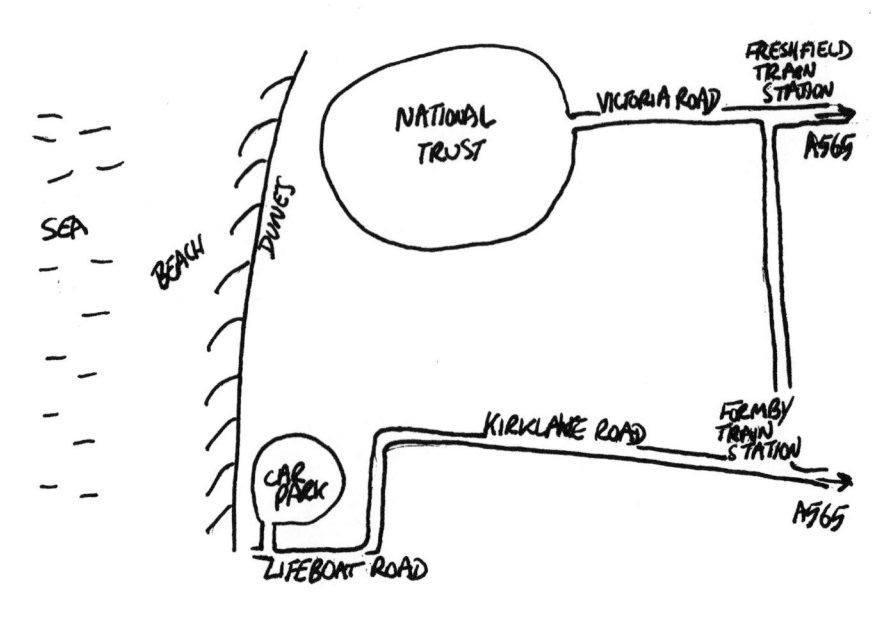

Though I would never recommend paying for car parking the National Trust part of Formby is amazing. The forest walks have a sizzling Mediterranean feel in the summer, while some of the red squirrels are friendly enough to eat... nuts out of your hand.

You can either head to Formby Point's National Trust property and pay for car parking (unless you are an NT member, in which case parking is free).

Alternatively, work your way round to a free car park near Formby Point Caravan Park on Lifeboat Road.

Fun rating: 4/5
Activity type: Outdoor play
Duration: Two hours
Address: Lifeboat Rd, Formby, Merseyside L37 2EB
or National Trust, Victoria Road, Formby, L37 1LJ
Age range: 3+
What will cost you more?
Car parking: Free (apart from National Trust)
Food and drink: Possible ice-cream van at National Trust site

NOTES:

This book would not have been possible without the family and friends who came out with me on some brilliant days out.

I would like to thank all of those people for spending time with me and my children. It means so much. Not all of these people are pictured in this book but, of those who are (including mam and dad who sneaked in), thanks must go to Anna Byrom and the following children (most are not mine):

Betsy Byrom
Minnie Byrom
Quentin Byrom
Teddy Cook
Archie Johnstone
Daniel Metcalfe
Georgia Metcalfe
Hayden Speak
Seamus Villa
Kitty Ward-Dooley

Gisburn Forest

EXTRA VENUE: "Exhilarating trails through forests, quarries and marsh land will put you through your paces in a day you will never forget"

IF you like cycling, then taking your kids mountain biking for the first time is a very proud moment – and it just so happens that one of Britain's most awesome and scenic courses is here in Lancashire.

Make no mistake – the main course is tough. It has bumps, steps and ramps around every corner. But, even if you can't stay in the saddle, the views across vastly differing terrain are worth the effort. Most competent adults can't complete every section but there is still a huge amount of fun to be had. However, the easy route is nothing more than a cycle track along a country road - and that's where the kids will build their confidence.

If you are taking teenage kids on the main route, be warned that some of the climbs are steep and in warm weather are incredibly energy sapping, especially if you are on heavy steel bikes. All routes are really well signposted so don't worry about a map – just stick to your route colour. There are signs at the (free) car park saying thieves have targeted cars in the past, so don't leave any valuables.

Fun rating: 4/5
Activity type: Mountain biking
Duration: Two to three hours
Age range: 10+ (Blue trail suitable for good cyclists 7+)
Address: Stephen Park, Gisburn Forest, Slaidburn, BB7 4TS
What will cost you more? Car Parking: Free

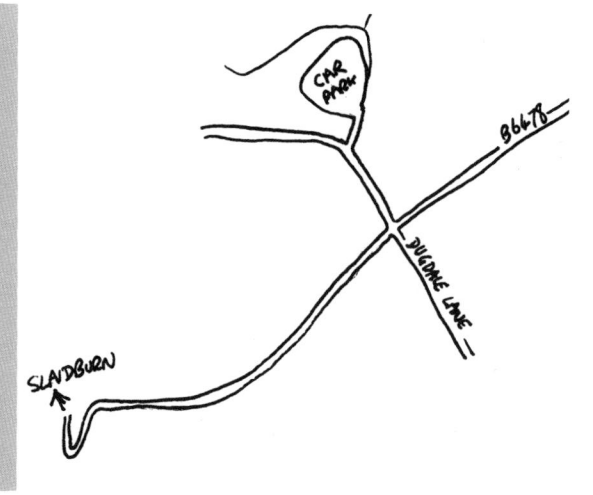